MESSAGES TO THE HEART

Reflections of Beauty and Truth

To The Ruschers,

From our I to yours,

Elise and Phil Okrend

Elise and Phil Okrend

Dedicated to Jordan and Josh. May all your dreams come true.

Cover and text design by Victoria Primicias
Production design by Brit Svensson-Dotson
Photograph of Elise and Phil Okrend by Serena Dawn Boggs
Copyright©2013 Mixedblessing, Inc.
Art ©2013 by Elise Okrend
Inspirational Passages ©2013 by Phil Okrend
MixedBlessing, Inc.
P.O. Box 8551, Asheville, NC 28814
919-847-7944

elise@eliseokrend.com
www.eliseokrend.com/messagestotheheart
www.messagestotheheart.com
www.steppingstonescoaching.com

ISBN: 978-0-9651475-1-4

CONTENTS

INTRODUCTION

This book was written for you.

We all are creators. Although some people create through art, through words, through music, we all can consciously create the depth and direction of our lives. As an artist is called from an inner drive and vision to create an image, what if you followed a call to create your vision of what an authentic and true life would be? It is this process that has led to the creation of Messages to the Heart.

This book was born from an organic pairing of one couple's creative passion. As an artist, Elise Okrend uses pastels to portray scenes of light, clouds, mountains, lakes and sacred places. Her desire is to foster a sense of peace and calmness for the viewer. As Elise was producing paintings for her gallery in Asheville, North Carolina, she previewed her work by posting the art to social media sites. At the same time, in his work as a life and business coach, Phil Okrend often shared his observations about change and empowerment on social media sites.

As sometimes the best things in life are unexpected, one day Phil was looking for an appropriate image to post with a thought he had written. He saw one of Elise's paintings on her post, and it seemed perfect for the idea he was trying to convey. From that first post, came many more. Elise and Phil found that the combination of art and words was powerful, and the feedback was positive and encouraging. People commented on the beauty and effect that the words and images had for them. It is from those posts that this book was created.

The intention with Messages to the Heart is to help open a door for you where peace, clarity, joy and purpose can come in. You are invited to use this book to inspire your own life vision. Take time to pause, meditate, journal or simply reflect on these pages. Also, when life becomes stressful, or there are challenges you need to pull yourself through, come back to this book, and come back to you.

This book was written for you.

Elise and Phil Okrend

Letting Go

If you don't know what you want, then let go of what you don't want. Perhaps when you empty yourself of outdated notions, limiting beliefs, what you thought you had to do from your conditioned mind, then the fruits of a new way will have the room to penetrate. It is much like clearing the dirt and debris to plant a new garden. We fight with ourselves when we try to force ourselves to be a certain way, live up to life standards that weren't set by us in the first place. Feel what makes you come alive and do that, but first, empty out what is no longer true for you. When you let go, don't feel that you need to rush into a new way. Allow yourself to take the time to be. Trust, be patient. The new way will come.

Letting Go

Give up your expectations of what and who you think you have to be, and start to live from who you were meant to be. The former is exhausting and the latter is just natural. When you give up the struggle, you find the path that was waiting for you all along.

Forgiveness

Forgiving others is an empowering act as each one of us holds a mirror for the other. Whatever you criticize or don't accept in another is what you don't accept in yourself. The path to true joy, freedom and connection to others is through forgiveness, through letting go of whatever you think is upsetting you about another. It also allows you to let go of the past and live in the present moment, where all life, all vitality, all possibility exists. Forgiveness gives you the key to true freedom and to truly live.

Surrender

When you surrender to the calling of your soul, there is a relief as you let go of control. When the ego no longer calls the shots, the only thing that matters is trust, belief, faith, love. We are at the point when control over others, control to get money, possessions, status has been fully played out and leaves you feeling alone, in a battle. That way is tiresome, old and exhausting. The new paradigm, and it has always been at the core of you, is trust through and through. No fighting, no games, no manipulation, no impatience. Just a calm knowing of your unique talents and using them to uplift others, to heal, to inspire, to give. It is filled with a patience that it will all work out and each moment becomes alive with these things.

Truth

When you clear yourself from a past that doesn't serve you anymore, you open yourself to a future that will. Stay present, pay attention. Ask yourself what are the situations and who are the people who reflect who you are. Do they reflect your values, your passions, your talents, what you uniquely have to offer? When you are clear on these questions, obstacles will just be detours and will not derail you for long. Stay true to who you are. Your future will be built from that.

Truth

On the other side of darkness is light, harmony and love. You don't need to look too far. You just need to open your eyes. It will always be there.

Feeling Alive

In the presence of aliveness, creative ideas happen spontaneously. They don't need to be forced. Find that place that makes you feel alive and spend time there. The answers will come.

Feeling Alive

If you don't allow yourself to feel genuine sadness, then you never allow yourself to get to the light and joy waiting for you at the other end.

Purpose

Each one of us has a purpose, a destiny. We each have a time when that purpose will manifest. You can not choose that time, that time chooses you. It is your job to recognize when that time is calling you. You can not prematurely put your actions into motion when the time isn't right, for then it is just your ego wanting control. Listen for the time, and then act. You will know when it is time.

Destiny

These three things will help you on your journey: Heal the Past, Live the Present, Dream the Future. **Heal the past** - See what the old stories and patterns are costing you in your life. You will know who and what you need to forgive. You will see that dealing with pain and discomfort now is better than having the past own you for "what you resist persists." **Live the present** - Your life only exists in this moment. The more you place your attention on what is in front of you, the more you will feel alive, energized and resourceful. **Dream the future** - Imagine an inspiring future where you are at your best, happy, fulfilled, contributing, engaged in life. From that vision, you will know what steps will either lead you there or will take you away from it. Practice these three things and you will find the path that has been waiting for you.

Choices

It is hard to draw water from a stone, but when you are near an ocean, it is easy. Know the difference between the people who are stones and oceans in your life. The stones will feel strained, you will work hard to get very little. When you are near oceans, there will be flow and ease. You won't have to work so hard and things happen on their own. There is a flow to life if you get out of your own way. As long as you know what you want, don't spend too much time near the stones. Go to the oceans. Even if the stones seem appealing, you will know if it always feels like an uphill battle. Drop your preconceived notions of who the right people should be in your life. Go towards what feels good, and spend time there. Trust.

Choices

The unknown future that has the capacity to fulfill your values is always the better course than a known past that no longer serves you or reflects who you are. You have the power to choose. You have the right to thrive.

Choices

Keep making choices. The only time you ever fail is when you stop choosing. Nothing is certain in life and neither do your choices give you certainty. However, your choices give you a navigation system. If you don't like the results you are getting from your choices, you now have the contrast to look at, to guide you to what would be better for you. But never stop choosing. If you never plant the seeds, you will never grow the garden. Keep choosing, and keep growing.

Consciousness

When your illusions start to fall apart, things can get uncomfortable, and facing the truth and responding to the realities of truth can also be uncomfortable. There will be discomfort either way. In terms of relativity, facing truth will lead to empowerment, growth, purpose, fulfillment. Staying in the illusion will lead to an inner dying or denial and living in the past. Choose truth and you will become free.

Higher Self

The death of the ego is the liberation of the soul.

Passion

Your talent, your passion, your potential lie all within you, and that is what is real. Don't determine your capability from something that you did in the past if that project, business, career is no longer representative of your growth. Don't ignore what is trying to get your attention. The next chapter of your life is determined by that deep yearning inside. When the past achievement becomes stale and repetitive, know that it is time to move on. We were intended to grow, to contribute from who we are, in our soul. Sometimes the seeds germinate in different stages, different time periods. Pay attention to that and pay attention to numbness, burnout and staleness when that occurs. Let go of what no longer works to allow what will work come through from within you.

Oneness

Imagine a new story:
Instead of consumerism - humanism,
Instead of greed - giving,
Instead of competition - cooperation,
Instead of conflict - coexistence,
Instead of fear - love,
Instead of sleeping - awakening,
Instead of control - surrender,
Instead of holding tightly - letting go,
Instead of feeling alone - feeling that we are one.
The truth is that this story has begun.
Let it live into our consciousness.

Trust

What is it to radiate love? What is it to radiate peace?
Let the clouds of illusion lift from your eyes. All the fears you
thought were real were just distractions from you realizing your
strength, your beauty, your purpose. Allow a sense of trust
to rise above and lead you to a better way. The illusions you
thought were real will crumble as you stop giving them power.
They will melt away and you will see the path. Follow the sun
and if you don't see it right away, feel your way there, listen
and trust. It will get brighter. It will get warmer.

Trust

If you want love, look within.

If you want peace, look within.

If you want satisfaction, look within.

If you want to be in harmony with others, look within.

If you want to be free of distraction, look within.

If you want to honor your truth, look within.

There is no reason to look anywhere else. All that you need is within. You were just looking in the wrong place.

Trust

If you let go of the veil of anxiety and apprehension, love can penetrate. It has no choice as that is your natural state. All else is conditioning and illusory. Love is the only real thing. Remember that the next time you feel anxiety creeping in.

Beauty

If you bring beauty into your life, then you bring beauty into the world.

Beauty

The world is full of beautiful landscapes and vistas, natural places that evoke feelings of reverence and awe. This natural beauty, what nature intended is also inside of you. When you understand that you are part of this nature, then you know that you have been blessed with gifts to express and touch others with. All fear, shame, guilt, doubt is just conditioning built from fear that tries to undermine you from seeing this truth. When you see it, know it is false and it will disappear as you no longer give it power.

Positivity

Have a mindset of positive expectancy when you set intentions and take steps to reach your goals and vision, but don't expect things to happen the exact way you want it. Then attachment sets in, takes you out of the present moment, and sets up a negative yearning when things don't go exactly as you plan or want them. Maybe there is another plan for you that is better than you thought, but you don't see it when you are too attached to one way. There is a greater plan for all of us when we learn to get out of our own way. Set your intention, take steps and enjoy your life. Something greater will come. Just trust it.

Lessons

If you could see your life as a perpetual place of learning and growth, then you can see that all your perceived setbacks, misfortunes, accidents, betrayals are merely signs to help you pay attention to what you haven't been paying attention to. When you take the time to reflect, you will be able to learn and grow. When you react to a perceived negative occurrence, you just continue that pattern. Open your eyes to a new way of seeing life because as you change your mind, you change your life.

Lessons

Many times new direction is forged from setback, disappointment and even tragedy. It is in those times that our character is tested and what calls into our souls is the essence of who we are. We are not here to focus just on comfort, playing it safe, playing it small. We are here to grow, learn, evolve. Other people will test us, conditions will test us, and even mother nature will test us. Out of these tests can come resiliency, determination and the coming together with others to find better ways, to move beyond the past. When you are in the midst of a challenging situation, don't despair, look ahead, and build a new, better way that may very well take you from here to the stars.

Healing

When the Outer Shell collapses, the Inner Heart is exposed to the light.

Change

A Cycle of Change: A storm can free your desire, your calmness can free your wisdom, your actions can free your destiny.

Present Moment

It is only in the present moment that you can enjoy your life. Being in the present moment gives you the open space to be receptive to new ideas and to hear the calling of your intuition. When you are in the present moment, you will know because you will be calm and it won't matter what is going on around you. If you are anxious or worried, you can never be in the present moment. When you find yourself in that place, take deep breaths, notice your body and start to let go. The cost of being out of the present moment is your joy and happiness. This is too important for you to forsake. Come back to the present moment and truly live.

Belief

When you believe in someone, you see them at their greatest potential, and you stand by them in their dreams, their insecurities, their triumphs, their setbacks. Life presents us with a continuous ladder of learning and growth. People are more likely to climb and continue to climb that ladder when others believe in them. Belief in others empowers them.

Who do you need to believe in including yourself?

Taking Steps

A comfort zone is an illusion of the mind that is used to keep it safe. No stepping out means no risk of rejection or ridicule, but the cost of that is not realizing your own fulfillment and potential. Ultimately the world will miss out on what you have to offer. When the feeling of fitting in, playing it safe is more important than your own life path, question that feeling. If you are a creator, your path will be filled with both missteps and triumphs, stumbling and learning. But as you take the steps, the next steps will open up for you, and as you progress, the novice will become the expert. Accept your life journey and move past the comfort zones. It is that important.

Strength

Life presents you with opportunities to find the strength you didn't know you had. When you find yourself in challenges or opposition, pull the strength out from deep inside you. It will come.

Faith

Miracles are natural occurrences and they can only happen from a receptive mind, not from a fearful mind. A receptive mind is natural and true. A fearful one is not natural and is illusory.

Self Worth

None of us are perfect, and yet all of us are deserving of love and understanding. We don't let ourselves be who we really are because we think others won't like it. But the truth is that others won't like it when they can't tell who you are and what you say really reflects who you are. That just leads to cynicism, distrust and fakeness over time. We need to give others permission to be exactly who they are so we can be who we are. No one is perfect, and yet we are all perfect in our imperfections. That is the human experience. We are here to love, learn, grow, be ourselves and know that our being here is our ticket to self worth. As we accept that and believe that, we build true authentic bonds of connection with others. All the striving to be something we are not in order to get self worth is a losing game that eventually catches up with people. You can only be an act for so long. It is your vulnerability which will make you strong and make you soar. Be yourself and be proud.

Self Worth

There is only one essential assumption to make in life. That is **You Are Worthy.** By understanding the truth of that, you understand that you do not need to prove anything, control anything, force anything. All you have to do is share what you already are with others and you will thrive. To believe otherwise is false to your true nature and causes needless pain and suffering for you and others. When you know you are worthy, you know that you do not lack anything and you are truly abundant. You are here to grow, share, learn and love. All the other stuff is just conditioning and learned behavior. All you need to do is let go of those falsities and come back to the truth of your worth.

Abundance

How to develop an abundance mentality. Instead of asking yourself what you are here to get, ask yourself, what are you here to give.

Character

Don't be ashamed of heartache, pain, setback or struggle. They have the means to shape you to forge courage, truth and to better serve others with the wisdom you gain from going through it. Each trial you face and overcome is a step of empowerment for yourself and others.

Wisdom

Listen to the calm, inner voice inside. It has all the wisdom you will ever need.

ART TITLES

BIO

As two creative souls passionate about the healing arts, Phil and Elise Okrend founded a successful greeting card company, MixedBlessing, in 1990 based on messages of peace, tolerance and diversity. The story behind their company was featured in national media such as The Wall Street Journal, USA Today and Good Morning America. Their greeting card business success allowed the couple to diversify further into individual passions. Elise now pursues her artistic callings in healing and mindful pastel paintings in her art gallery space in Asheville, North Carolina and in the permanent collection of hospitals, offices and residences. Phil helps hundreds of clients as a certified life and business coach, incorporating writing, public speaking and original reflective music into his practice.

Phil and Elise currently make their home in the mountains of North Carolina where they enjoy hiking, kayaking and being in nature. They have two sons, Jordan and Josh, and a blue eyed dog, Maya.

CPSIA information can be obtained
at www.ICGtesting.com
Printed in the USA
BVXC01n0238140814
362695BV00002B/2